Sequoyah Talking Leaves

A Play about the Cherokee Syllabary

Written by Wim Coleman and Pat Perrin
Illustrated by Siri Weber Feeney

RED
CHAIR
•PRESS•

Please visit our website at **www.redchairpress.com** for more high-quality products for young readers.

 EDUCATORS: Find FREE lesson plans and a Readers' Theater script for this book at www.redchairpress.com/free-activities.

About the Authors

Wim Coleman and **Pat Perrin** are a husband and wife who write together. Their more-than-100 publications include plays, stories, articles, essays, books, classroom materials, and mainstream fiction. Wim has a BFA in Theatre Arts and an MAT in English and Education from Drake University. Pat has a BA in English from Duke, an MA in Liberal Studies from Hollins University, and a PhD in Art Theory and Criticism from the University of Georgia. Both have classroom teaching experience. For 13 years they lived in the beautiful Mexican town of San Miguel de Allende, where they created and managed a scholarship program for at-risk students under the auspices of San Miguel PEN. Some of their stories draw on Mexican myth and tradition. Their highly-praised works for young readers include award-winning historical fiction, popular collections of plays, and a "nonfiction" book about unicorns.

Sequoyah and His Talking Leaves

Publisher's Cataloging-In-Publication Data
(Prepared by The Donohue Group, Inc.)

Coleman, Wim.
Sequoyah and his talking leaves : a play about the Cherokee syllabary / by Wim Coleman and Pat Perrin ; illustrated by Siri Weber Feeney.

p. : ill. ; cm. -- (Setting the stage for fluency)

Summary: A dramatization about how the Native American, Sequoyah, set about creating a written Cherokee language, helping to preserve the tribe's history and culture even today. Includes special book features for further study and a special section for teachers and librarians.
Interest age level: 009-012.
Includes bibliographical references.
ISBN: 978-1-939656-36-0 (lib. binding/hardcover)
ISBN: 978-1-939656-35-3 (pbk.)
ISBN: 978-1-939656-37-7 (eBk)

1. Cherokee language--Writing--Juvenile drama. 2. Sequoyah, 1770?-1843--Juvenile drama. 3. Cherokee Indians--Juvenile drama. 4. Sequoyah, 1770?-1843--Drama. 5. Cherokee Indians--Drama. 6. Children's plays, American. 7. Historical drama. I. Perrin, Pat. II. Feeney, Siri Weber. III. Title.

PS3553.O47448 Se 2014
[Fic]   2013956253

This series first published by:
Red Chair Press LLC   PO Box 333   South Egremont, MA 01258-0333

Printed in the United States of America

1 2 3 4 5 18 17 16 15 14

TABLE OF CONTENTS

INTRODUCTION

Sequoyah was a Native American Cherokee. Like most of his people, he was illiterate. That means that he could not read and write. But there was no written Cherokee language for anyone to read or write. Not until Sequoyah invented it himself.

Sequoyah saw papers written in English. He quickly understood what written language could do. He also realized that words are made up of separate sounds. Those sounds are repeated in different order to make up different words. We call them "syllables." Sequoyah invented a writing system based on syllables.

We call Sequoyah's writing system a "syllabary." It was easy to learn and use. Sequoyah soon became world famous for his work.

Never in recorded history has anyone accomplished what Sequoyah did. No one else in an illiterate society ever invented a writing system. This play tells what we know about his story.

THE CAST OF CHARACTERS

Historians: 1 and 2

Sequoyah: a Cherokee

Cherokee men: 1, 2, 3

Sally: Sequoyah's wife

Ayoka: Sequoyah's daughter

Cherokee conjurors: 1, 2, 3, 4

Reverend Samuel Worcester: a Christian missionary

Teesee: Sequoyah's son

Setting: Southern part of the United States

Time: The early 1800s

5

SCENE ONE

Historian 1: We're not sure when, where, or how our story began…

Historian 2: Possibly in a shop in the Cherokee village of Wills Town, Alabama.

Historian 1: It was somewhere between 1809 and 1820. We really don't know the year.

Historian 2: A man named Sequoyah was a **metalsmith**. One day he paused from his work. He stopped to talk with some friends. One of them was looking at a newspaper.

Sequoyah: What is that strange sheet?

Cherokee 1: I don't know, but I've seen sheets like this before. A white man threw it off his wagon as he drove through town.

Cherokee 2: And it's covered with all kinds of crazy marks.

Cherokee 3: Thousands of them.

Sequoyah: Here—let me see it.

Historian 1: His friends handed him the newspaper.

Sequoyah: Why, it's a talking leaf. I've heard of such things, but I've never seen one before.

Cherokee 1: I've seen white men staring at sheets like this for hours at a time.

Cherokee 2: They say that these marks are messages that speak. They call it "reading."

Cherokee 3: It's powerful magic, I've heard. They say it's a gift to the white man from the Great Spirit.

Sequoyah: That sounds foolish. Why would the Great Spirit give magic to white men and not to us Cherokee?

Cherokee 3: Well, that's what I've heard.

Cherokee 2: I don't believe it. This "reading"—it's all pretend. White men stare at these sheets just to puzzle us Cherokee. They want us to believe they have magic that we don't have.

Sequoyah: More foolishness. Why, it's easy to see how it works. Here, let me show you.

Historian 2: Sequoyah didn't have pen, paper, or ink.

Historian 1: He'd never even heard of such things. So he picked up a flat piece of stone and a knife.

Sequoyah: Somebody say something.

Cherokee 3: Like what?

Sequoyah: Anything at all.

Cherokee 3: All right. I caught a fish yesterday.

Sequoyah: Perfect.

Historian 2: Sequoyah began to scratch **symbols** on the stone with his knife.

Sequoyah: This mark means *I*. This one means *caught*. This one means *a*. This one means *fish*. This one means *yesterday*. You see? Anyone who knows what each of these marks mean could understand this message just by looking at it. Now if we just had a mark for every word that we Cherokee ever say…

Cherokee 1: *(laughing)* You really are the craziest man I ever met!

Cherokee 2: Do you really think talking leaves work this way?

Cherokee 3: It's magic, I tell you.

Cherokee 2: And I say it's all just pretend.

Cherokee 1: Let's stop talking about it—or else we'll *all* go crazy.

SCENE TWO

Historian 1: That's how some people say it happened, anyway. We historians don't know for sure.

Historian 2: There are very few known facts about Sequoyah's life.

Historian 1: We think he was born around 1778.

Historian 2: We do know that his mother was named Wurteh. We think his father was a white or half-white man named Nathaniel Gist.

Historian 1: He never knew his father.

Historian 2: We know that Sequoyah was lame in one leg. But we don't know why.

Historian 1: We do know one important fact about him. Sequoyah could not stop thinking about those "talking leaves."

Historian 2: At first, he tried using symbols. He tried to come up with a symbol for every word in the Cherokee language.

Sequoyah: It's no use—there are simply too many words. I can't make symbols for all of them. Even if I could, there would be far too many for people to learn.

Historian 1: Then, slowly, something dawned on him…

Sequoyah: Why, many words use the same sounds! There are far fewer sounds than there are words! I need to discover every sound used in Cherokee speech. Then I'll be able to create marks for all of the sounds.

Historian 2: Many people call Sequoyah's writing system an alphabet. Actually, it was based on the individual sounds of words, or syllables—so it was really a syllabary.

SCENE THREE

Historian 1: Sequoyah kept thinking about the talking leaves. Soon, he gave up farming and smithing. He devoted all his time to inventing a Cherokee form of writing.

Historian 2: He built himself a hut in the woods. There, he could work in peace and quiet.

Historian 1: He bought paper and ink. He learned to make his own quill pens.

Historian 2: Everybody thought he was lazy or crazy or worse. Even his wife, Sally, was worried.

Sally: You used to work at smithing instead of doing this.

Sequoyah: That was a long time ago. This is important.

Sally: What you're doing now is useless. Or worse than useless. Evil, maybe. Some people say so.

Sequoyah: *(showing her a piece of paper)* Look at these two marks. Do you know what they mean?

Sally: They don't mean anything.

Sequoyah: They make sounds.

Sally: They're silent to me.

Sequoyah: They won't be in a moment. *(pointing to the marks)* This one says *sal*. This one says *ly*. Together they say *Sal-ly*. Your name. Say it.

Sally: *(interested in spite of herself)* Sally.

Sequoyah: There. From now on, you'll hear your name whenever you see these two marks together. It will ring out loud in your ear. You won't be able to stop it. It will be like someone calling out to you. But our daughter is coming. Let's not argue in front of her.

Historian 1: Their daughter Ayoka was just a little girl.

Historian 2: Her eyes lit up when she saw all the little pieces of paper.

Ayoka: Oh, look, Mother! Father is writing your name! *Sally!*

Sally: *(to Ayoka)* But how do you know...?

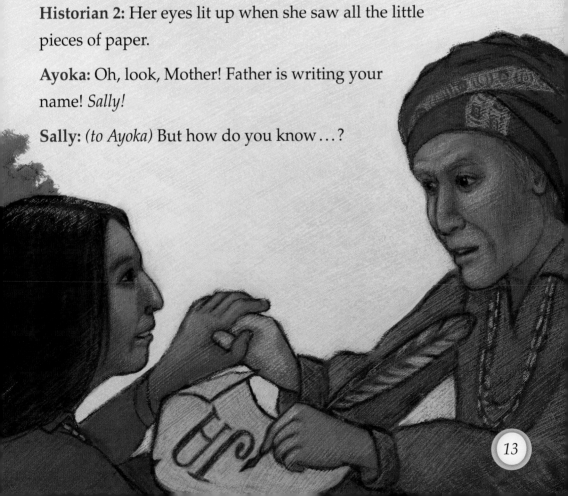

Historian 1: Ayoka knew because she'd been helping her father all along.

Historian 2: Every day, she went out and listened to people talk. She memorized the sounds they would make.

Historian 1: Then she would go to her father's hut and repeat the sounds to him. He would make symbols for those sounds.

Sequoyah: That's seven sounds you've brought today, Ayoka! The most you've ever gotten at one time!

Ayoka: And you've made marks for all of them. They're so pretty to look at.

Sequoyah: Do you like going out searching for sounds, daughter?

Ayoka: Oh, yes, it's a lot of fun—like catching little birds.

Sequoyah: Not birds. And nothing little. We're trying to catch and tame a much bigger animal. It's something rare, beautiful, and strong.

Ayoka: And wild?

Sequoyah: Very wild indeed. Our Cherokee language has been running free for—who knows how long? Hundreds of years, maybe thousands.

Ayoka: Why do we want to tame it?

Sequoyah: Why do we want to tame a wild horse? So we can ride it. So it can help us work. So it can be our friend in more ways than we can imagine.

Ayoka: But maybe our language is happy being wild.

Sequoyah: Yes, I've wondered that myself. It would be wicked to tame a splendid creature that loves its liberty. Some animals just **pine away** in captivity.

Ayoka: Like an eagle.

Sequoyah: Or a deer.

Ayoka: Or a wolf.

Sequoyah: Or a bear.

Ayoka: A bear more than anything.

Sequoyah: If you put them in a cage they grow sad. You can't tie them to a rope and order them about. They stop eating and die. But I don't think our language is like any of those animals.

Ayoka: No?

Sequoyah: It doesn't run away into the forest to hide from people. It spends all its time among us Cherokee. We don't even notice it's there. It keeps slipping in and out of our lips and ears, just like now. It's here while you and I are talking. I think it wants to be our friend. It wants to learn our ways. But let's get back to work. Seven sounds, and seven marks! Why, I believe we could get seven times seven words out of these sounds. How many does that come to?

Ayoka: Forty-nine.

Sequoyah: Very good.

Ayoka: Oh, Father, do you really think we can do that? Can we make that many words out of just seven symbols?

Sequoyah: Let's cut them apart and move them around. We'll see what they can do.

Historian 1: While Sequoyah worked in his hut, trouble was brewing among the tribe.

Historian 2: The Cherokee **conjurors** heard about what Sequoyah was doing.

Historian 1: They summoned him to a meeting. But it was more like a trial.

Conjuror 1: People say you practice evil magic.

Sequoyah: That's a lie.

Conjuror 2: That's for us to decide.

Conjuror 3: They say you make leaves that talk.

Sequoyah: There's nothing magical about talking leaves. It's something learned. It's the same way a boy learns to shoot an arrow. It's how a scout learns his way through thick forest. It's the way a little girl learns to milk a cow.

Conjuror 4: We believe you're controlled by a *shee-leh*.

Sequoyah: An evil demon?

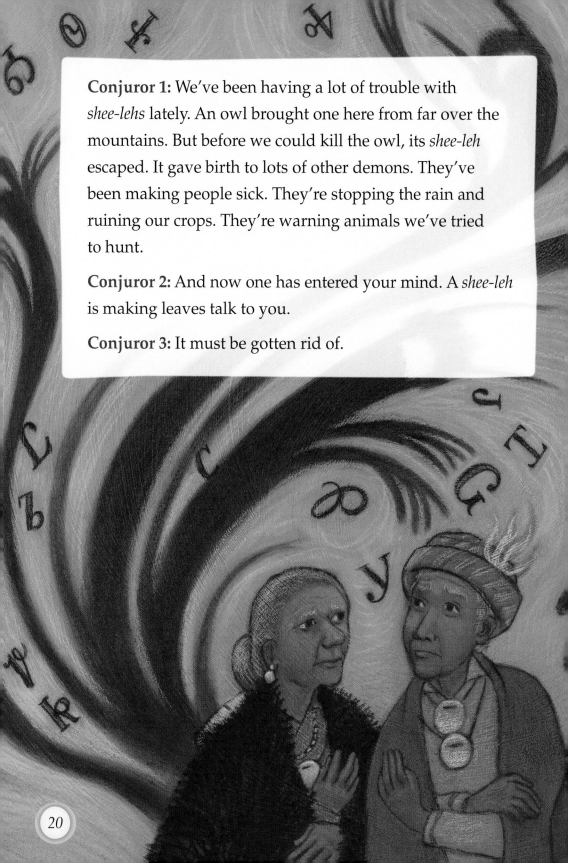

Conjuror 1: We've been having a lot of trouble with *shee-lehs* lately. An owl brought one here from far over the mountains. But before we could kill the owl, its *shee-leh* escaped. It gave birth to lots of other demons. They've been making people sick. They're stopping the rain and ruining our crops. They're warning animals we've tried to hunt.

Conjuror 2: And now one has entered your mind. A *shee-leh* is making leaves talk to you.

Conjuror 3: It must be gotten rid of.

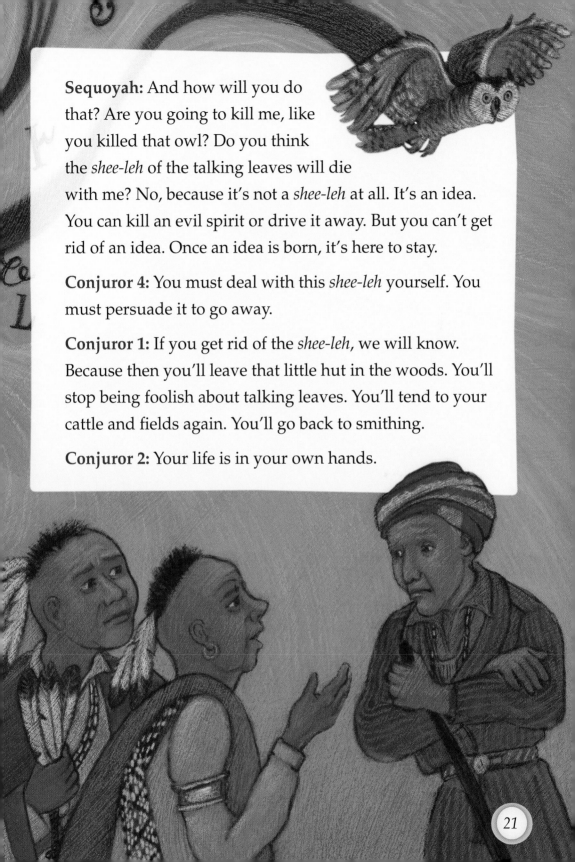

Sequoyah: And how will you do that? Are you going to kill me, like you killed that owl? Do you think the *shee-leh* of the talking leaves will die with me? No, because it's not a *shee-leh* at all. It's an idea. You can kill an evil spirit or drive it away. But you can't get rid of an idea. Once an idea is born, it's here to stay.

Conjuror 4: You must deal with this *shee-leh* yourself. You must persuade it to go away.

Conjuror 1: If you get rid of the *shee-leh*, we will know. Because then you'll leave that little hut in the woods. You'll stop being foolish about talking leaves. You'll tend to your cattle and fields again. You'll go back to smithing.

Conjuror 2: Your life is in your own hands.

Historian 1: Now, what do we suppose happened next?

Historian 2: Well, we do know that Sequoyah disobeyed the tribal conjurors. He kept right on working on his writing in his lonely hut.

Historian 1: But one day something terrible happened.

Historian 2: We don't know where he was or what he was doing at the time. Perhaps he was away from his hut, hunting game. Perhaps he was gathering berries.

Historian 1: When he returned, he found his hut burned to the ground. All his work was destroyed along with it.

Historian 2: We can imagine his wife and daughter joining him there. They would be looking with horror at the smoking, ashy ruin.

Ayoka: Who could have done this?

Sequoyah: Never mind who did it. My work is ruined.

Sally: It's not ruined. I won't let it be ruined.

Sequoyah: I thought you didn't want me doing this work.

23

Sally: That was before this happened. The conjurors did this to you. And I don't like the conjurors. Whenever they see something or somebody they don't like, they start shouting, "Shee-leh, shee-leh!" And some people are stupid enough to believe them.

Sequoyah: You don't believe in *shee-lehs*?

Sally: Of course I do. My mother was killed by one. But there can't be as many *shee-lehs* in the world as the conjurors say there are. If there were, we'd choke on them. The conjurors are small-minded men. They hate the sight or smell of anything new or good in the world. They don't like your talking leaves. Well, that's enough to convince me that talking leaves are good. Let's get back to work on these talking leaves of yours—the three of us.

Sequoyah: But all my papers are burned. I'm sure I can't remember more than half of the marks.

Ayoka: I can remember them—every one. And the sounds too—but maybe not all of the sounds.

Sally: You tell me which sounds are missing. I'll go track them down. Meanwhile, husband, you start rebuilding this hut. And daughter, you start writing down those marks.

SCENE SEVEN

Historian 1: Before long, Sequoyah and his family had 86 symbols. It was a complete syllabary. The symbols represented every single sound or syllable in the Cherokee language.

Historian 2: They also knew how to put the symbols together into words.

Historian 1: Quietly and secretly, they taught their syllabary to some of their friends.

Historian 2: Then, one day in 1821, Sequoyah called a meeting. He gathered all the Cherokee in Wills Town together.

Sequoyah: Friends, neighbors, and enemies too—I have succeeded in my quest. With precious help from my wife and daughter, I have succeeded. We can make leaves talk.

(The crowd gasps)

Sequoyah: Now I will prove it to you. Here, standing in front of you, are 10 of my friends. They've learned to write their thoughts on paper in our Cherokee language. I'll send each of them home with pen, ink, and paper. All alone, each of them will write a message. It doesn't matter what they write. No one else can know what it is. They will seal their messages with wax. Then they will exchange messages. You will all watch this exchange carefully, so we can't trick you. They will open up each other's messages and read them.

Historian 1: Sequoyah's pupils went to their homes to write their messages. The crowd waited breathlessly to see what would happen.

Historian 2: The pupils soon returned from their houses.

Historian 1: They exchanged their messages. Then they read them to each other perfectly.

Historian 2: All the Cherokee of Wills Town went wild with excitement. They sang and danced and prepared a feast to celebrate.

Historian 1: All except the conjurors. They stood apart from all the others. They crossed their arms and frowned.

Historian 2: At last, the conjurors began to murmur among themselves. Then they stepped forward to speak with Sequoyah.

Conjuror 1: We demand another talk with you. Matters are much more serious than we imagined.

Sequoyah: Then you still believe my talking leaves are the work of some *shee-leh*?

Conjuror 2: We won't discuss that here. We must speak with you alone.

Sequoyah: Do you really think the talking leaves are evil? If you do and someone must die for it, take my life. Let my wife and daughter and friends live. Surely I'm the only one of us who is possessed by a *shee-leh*.

Conjuror 3: Say no more. Come with us.

Conjuror 4: Oh—and bring a pen and ink and leaves of paper with you.

Historian 1: We don't know just what happened next.

Historian 2: But we can imagine this scene. Sequoyah is standing in a clearing in the forest. He is surrounded by the frightening conjurors. Sequoyah wonders if he will return home alive.

Conjuror 1: Write a message for us. Something short and simple.

Historian 3: Sequoyah used a tree stump as a writing desk. He wrote quickly.

Conjuror 1: Now—let me see it.

Historian 1: Sequoyah handed the message to the head conjuror.

Conjuror 1: Now teach me to read it.

Sequoyah: *(with surprise)* Do you mean—tell you what it says?

Conjuror 1: No. Teach me how it works. Then I can tell what it says for myself.

Historian 2: The other conjurors gathered around them. Sequoyah taught the head conjuror the sound of every mark in the message.

Conjuror 1: I can read it now. It says, "Ꭲ ꙦꙎꝹr tꙆꙦ tꙅ ꞒꝌ Ꝺꝇ. Ꭲ ꝒiR Ꝺnd ꝆR Ꝺ fꝹTthfꝄⷈl 4riꝹnt tꙅ tꝒ CꝐrꙅkRR pRꙅpꙅ." I swear this to you all. I live and die a faithful servant to the Cherokee people.

Conjuror 2: Yes, I can read it too.

Conjuror 3: And I.

Conjuror 4: And I.

Conjuror 2: No wicked *shee-leh* would allow him to write such a message.

Conjuror 3: It must be a good spirit instead. Not an evil spirit.

Conjuror 1: I felt the presence of no spirit at all. I felt only the turning of mighty wheels in my brain. It was an amazing feeling. *(to Sequoyah)* Start teaching us now— right this very minute.

Sequoyah: Why?

Conjuror 1: Our magic has grown weaker. The white man's **missionaries** are determined to make us forget our own beliefs. They've succeeded all too well.

Conjuror 2: The youngest Cherokee have never learned any of our magic. Our ways are being forgotten.

Conjuror 3: We're old—all of us.

Conjuror 4: There's not a young conjuror left in Wills Town. There's not one in this whole territory.

Conjuror 1: We'll die off soon.

Conjuror 2: But your talking leaves can save us.

Conjuror 3: They can remind us always of who we Cherokee are.

Conjuror 4: We can write down all our secrets. We can share our dances and songs. We can give others our cures for madness and disease. We can tell about our ways of bringing rain and good hunting. We can record our spells to cast out evil spirits and invite good ones. We can save all our stories.

Conjuror 1: What's best about us will never die. Our knowledge will live forever. That way, the Cherokee people will live forever.

SCENE NINE

Historian 1: Within days, word spread among the Cherokee people. They heard about Sequoyah's talking leaves.

Historian 2: Everybody wanted to learn it—and thousands did.

Historian 1: It was easy to learn. It took only three or four days of lessons. Then people could read and write remarkably well with the new symbols.

Historian 2: Literacy spread like wildfire among the Cherokee.

Historian 1: Young men began writing letters to their sweethearts. They anxiously awaited letters in return.

Historian 2: The eastern Cherokee exchanged messages with other Cherokee in faraway Arkansas territory. People who had long been separated felt close to one another again.

Historian 1: In 1824, the Cherokee National Council awarded Sequoyah a medal for his achievement.

Historian 2: The Cherokee nation officially adopted the syllabary in 1825.

Historian 1: Before long, a new newspaper began using the syllabary. By 1828, the *Cherokee Phoenix* printed stories in the Cherokee language. It was read by Cherokee far and wide.

Historian 2: Everyone was happy with the talking leaves.

Historian 1: One day in 1825, a white man arrived. He met with Sequoyah.

Reverend Worcester: My name is Samuel Worcester—the Reverend Samuel Worcester.

Sequoyah: *(with distaste)* A missionary. There have been many here already.

Reverend Worcester: *(chuckling)* Yes, I thought you might not be happy about that. I speak Cherokee fairly well. We can talk together in your language.

Sequoyah: Why do you want to talk to me?

Reverend Worcester: I wouldn't miss the opportunity. You're the most honored and respected Cherokee alive. Perhaps the most honored and respected Indian in all of North America.

Sequoyah: That is something I don't believe.

Reverend Worcester: Do you have any idea what a truly amazing thing you've done—and how rare? Written languages grow slowly. They develop over hundreds or thousands of years. They need the help of countless people. As far as I know, you're very unusual in human history. You may be the only one to have created an alphabet or syllabary within a single lifetime. I believe that you are one of the greatest geniuses who ever lived.

Sequoyah: What is a **genius**?

Reverend Worcester: *(laughing)* If I were a genius, I could tell you. Sadly, I can't. *(pause)* I think your syllabary is useful to us. I've made arrangements to have the New Testament translated and printed in your language. A well-educated Cherokee is already at work on it. He's fluent in English and Ancient Greek. Soon, every Cherokee who can read will have a copy of it.

Sequoyah: I didn't realize that your people could use my work. If I had, I might never have started it.

Reverend Worcester: I don't think that's true. Anyway, there's nothing you can do about it. When a man creates something brilliant and wonderful, it's no longer his. It belongs to the world.

Historian 1: Sequoyah worried that the talking leaves meant to preserve the Cherokee way of life and Cherokee beliefs might now be used to change those things.

EPILOGUE

Historian 1: In 1829, the federal government moved Sequoyah and about 2,500 other Cherokee to Indian Territory in what is now Oklahoma. He settled near present-day Sallisaw where he built a log cabin.

Historian 2: Sequoyah spent much of the last part of his life writing a book.

Historian 1: What was it about?

Historian 2: He never let anyone read it. He said it told the story of the Cherokee people.

Historian 1: Perhaps he wrote of his own life too. All the things we don't know—written down in his own hand!

Historian 2: He took the pages with him on a trip to Mexico. He kept writing during the entire journey. By then, Sequoyah was old and ill. He died there in 1843, among the Cherokee of Mexico.

Historian 1: But what happened to the book? Where is it now?

Historian 2: Buried with him, it is said. But no one has ever been able to find his grave.

Historian 1: So this book is buried somewhere in northern Mexico. It is possibly the greatest story ever written by a Native American. And it's just waiting to be found.

conjuror: a magician

genius: an unusually smart person

literacy: the ability to read and write

metalsmith: a person skilled in working with metals

missionary: one who does religious work in a foreign country or place

pine away: suffer from a broken heart

symbol: a thing that stands for something else

Learn More about Sequoyah and the Cherokee

Books:

Wade, Mary Dodson. *Amazing Cherokee Writer Sequoyah*. Enslow Publishing, 2009.

Waxman, Laura Hamilton. *Sequoyah* (History Maker Biographies). Lerner, 2004.

Web Sites:

Sequoyah Birthplace Museum: contributions of Sequoyah to Cherokee history; www.sequoyahmuseum.org

Cherokee Nation Official Site: information about Sequoyah, the Cherokee language, and Cherokee history and culture; www.cherokee.org

Places:

The log cabin Sequoyah built near Sallisaw, Oklahoma, is still standing and open to the public as a national landmark. www.okhistory.org/sites/sequoyahcabin